am Spirit

THE SEATTLE SEAHAWKS

BY
MARK STEWART

Content Consultant
Jason Aikens

NORWOOD HOUSE PRESS

CHICAGO, ILLINOIS

Norwood House Press
P.O. Box 316598
Chicago, Illinois 60631

For information regarding Norwood House Press, please visit our website at:
www.norwoodhousepress.com or call 866-565-2900.

PHOTO CREDITS:
All photos courtesy of Getty Images except the following:
Topps, Inc. (7 both, 9, 20, 21, 22, 29, 34 both, 35 bottom left & right,
36, 37, 39, 40 top & bottom left, 41 top & bottom right, 43);
Black Book Partners Archive (14); Matt Richman (48 top).
Cover Photo: Otto Greule Jr./Getty Images
Special thanks to Topps, Inc.

Editor: Mike Kennedy
Designer: Ron Jaffe
Project Management: Black Book Partners, LLC.
Research: Evan Frankel
Special thanks to: Howard and Max Rossbach

LIBRARY OF CONGRESS CATALOGING-IN-PUBLICATION DATA

Stewart, Mark, 1960-
    The Seattle Seahawks / by Mark Stewart ; content consultant Jason Aikens.
        p. cm. -- (Team spirit)
    Includes bibliographical references and index.
    Summary: "Presents the history, accomplishments and key personalities of
the Seattle Seahawks football team. Includes timelines, quotes, maps,
glossary and websites"--Provided by publisher.
    ISBN-13: 978-1-59953-201-1 (library edition : alk. paper)
    ISBN-10: 1-59953-201-8 (library edition : alk. paper) 1. Seattle
Seahawks (Football team)--History--Juvenile literature. I. Aikens, Jason.
II. Title.
    GV956.S4S84 2008
    796.332'6409797772--dc22
                                                                    2008012778

COVER PHOTO: The Seahawks celebrate a touchdown during a 2007 game.

Table of Contents

SPORTS WORDS & VOCABULARY WORDS: In this book, you will find many words that are new to you. You may also see familiar words used in new ways. The glossary on page 46 gives the meanings of football words, as well as "everyday" words that have special football meanings. These words appear in **bold type** throughout the book. The glossary on page 47 gives the meanings of vocabulary words that are not related to football. They appear in ***bold italic type*** throughout the book.

Meet the Seahawks

What drives **professional** football players? Many will tell you that the thing they love best about their sport is the roar of the crowd when they score a touchdown, recover a **fumble**, or make an **interception**. The Seattle Seahawks certainly feel this way. Their fans are among the loudest and most supportive in the **National Football League (NFL)**.

To football fans in the Pacific Northwest, the Seahawks are a source of *intense* pride. Players are always amazed when they join the Seahawks. They realize that they are part of something much bigger than a professional football team.

This book tells the story of the Seahawks. They are a team that succeeds with strength, speed, and teamwork. The players who cheer from the sidelines are just as beloved as the stars who make great plays on the field. And each win is a victory for an entire region.

Quarterback Matt Hasselbeck huddles his teammates and calls a play during a 2007 game.

Way Back When

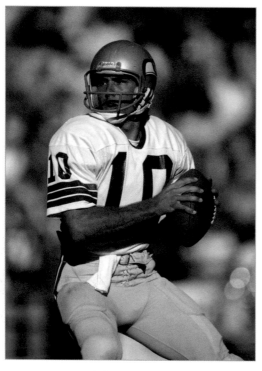

During the 1970s, the state of Washington wanted to be a "player" in the world of professional sports. The city of Seattle already had a basketball team, the Supersonics. Getting football and baseball teams, however, would take a big effort. In 1972, construction began on a new stadium called the Kingdome.

In 1974, the NFL awarded Seattle one of two new teams for the 1976 season. The Seahawks got to work on building a team.

Seattle selected unwanted players from other NFL teams, **drafted** a few college players, and held tryouts during the summer of 1976. The Seahawks' goal was to find a good quarterback who could lead them during their early years. Many players were invited to compete for the job. The man who won it rolled into camp in a broken-down Volkswagen Beetle. His name was Jim Zorn.

LEFT: Jim Zorn, Seattle's first great quarterback.
TOP RIGHT: Curt Warner
BOTTOM RIGHT: Kenny Easley

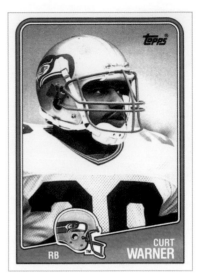

Zorn had a strong left arm and quick feet. He would need them with the Seahawks. Seattle's offensive line didn't always protect Zorn well, so he often found himself running away from defenders. His ability to move gave his receivers extra time to get open. Zorn's favorite target was Steve Largent, a **rookie** drafted by the Houston Oilers and then traded to the Seahawks. With Zorn, Largent, and running back Sherman Smith, Seattle had a good offense. The defense was another matter. The Seahawks allowed 30 or more points in half their games in their first season and finished with a record of 2–12.

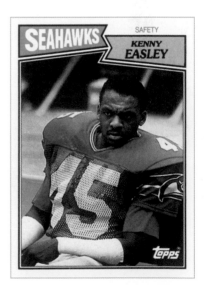

By the end of the 1970s, Zorn and Largent were one of the best passing combinations in the NFL. When Seattle's defense improved, the team began to show signs it could be a championship *contender*. In the 1980s, the Seahawks added three new stars, safety Kenny Easley, pass rusher Jacob Green, and running back Curt Warner. Also during the *decade*, Dave Krieg replaced Zorn as the team's quarterback. He led

the Seahawks all the way to the championship game of the **American Football Conference (AFC)** in 1983. Five years later, Seattle won the **AFC West** for the first time. Krieg, Warner, and Largent were joined by new stars Brian Blades and John L. Williams.

The Seahawks struggled during the 1990s. They had several good players, including Cortez Kennedy, Eugene Robinson, Joey Galloway, and Warren Moon. Unfortunately, they could not compete with powerful clubs in the AFC West, such as the Oakland Raiders and Denver Broncos. In 1999, the team hired Mike Holmgren as its head coach. He had led the Green Bay Packers to the **Super Bowl** twice and had won the big game once.

The Seahawks won the AFC West in Holmgren's first season. With their pride restored, the players began focusing on their coach's next goal. Holmgren would not be satisfied until Seattle made it to the Super Bowl.

LEFT: Steve Largent, the top receiver in Seahawks history.
ABOVE: Cortez Kennedy, a star for the team during the 1990s.

The Team Today

In 2002, the NFL changed its divisions for the first time since 1970. The Seahawks moved from the AFC to the **National Football Conference (NFC)**. Their new *rivals* were the San Francisco 49ers, St. Louis Rams, and Arizona Cardinals. In 2004, the Seahawks won the **NFC West**.

Seattle had a quick, hard-hitting defense and a very talented group of **blockers** on offense. Their job was to protect quarterback Matt Hasselbeck and open holes for running back Shaun Alexander. The Seahawks won 13 games in 2005, the most in the NFC. They rolled through the **playoffs** and made it to their first Super Bowl. They lost a close game to the Pittsburgh Steelers.

In the years since, the Seahawks have tried to keep the core of that great team together. They also added exciting new players. Today, the Seahawks have an excellent chance to win every time they step on the field. That makes the players and fans feel good—but they won't be satisfied until they win the Super Bowl.

Patrick Kerney and Lofa Tatupu, two of the stars who have helped Seattle build one of the NFL's best defenses.

Home Turf

The Seahawks played their first 24 seasons in the Kingdome. It was one of the noisiest stadiums in sports. The loud crowds gave the team a big boost, especially in close games.

In 2000, construction began on a new stadium on the site where the Kingdome used to be. Paul Allen, the team's owner, wanted a "perfect" stadium for his players and fans. To help this happen, he spent $160 million of his own personal fortune.

The new stadium opened in 2002. Many of the seats are covered, but the field is not. The roof was designed to reflect crowd noise onto the field. Much of that noise is made by fans in the Hawk's Nest, a special section where fans can stomp on the metal bleachers.

BY THE NUMBERS

- *The Seahawks' stadium has 67,000 seats for football.*
- *The stadium cost $430 million to build.*
- *The Seahawks lost to the Arizona Cardinals 24–13 in the stadium's first regular-season game.*

The roof on Seattle's stadium offers protection for some seats but leaves the field open to sunlight.

Dressed for Success

In 1975, Seattle's owners held a contest to choose the team's name. They received more than 20,000 entries from fans. The team decided on Seahawks. Seahawk is another name for the osprey, a bird that is native to the Pacific Northwest.

Seattle's helmet design shows a seahawk's head drawn in a traditional Native American style. The team's original colors were blue and forest green. These colors are familiar to people in the region, where the forests often stretch down to the water's edge. Silver and white were the Seahawks' other main colors.

In 2002, the team changed its colors to match its new stadium. The Seahawks started using two shades of blue and a brighter shade of green. The team thought about changing its helmet color from silver to blue. The Seahawks asked their fans to vote, and they picked blue. It was the first time an NFL team let its fans decide a uniform color.

Dave Krieg models the team's uniform from the 1980s.

UNIFORM BASICS

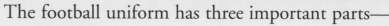

The football uniform has three important parts—

- Helmet
- Jersey
- Pants

Helmets used to be made out of leather, and they did not have facemasks—ouch! Today, helmets are made of super-strong plastic. The uniform top, or jersey, is made of thick fabric. It fits snugly around a player so that tacklers cannot grab it and pull him down. The pants come down just over the knees.

There is a lot more to a football uniform than what you see on the outside. Air can be pumped inside the helmet to give it a snug, padded fit. The jersey covers shoulder pads, and sometimes a rib protector called a flak jacket. The pants include pads that protect the hips, thighs, *tailbone*, and knees.

Football teams have two sets of uniforms— one dark and one light. This makes it easier to tell two teams apart on the field. Almost all teams wear their dark uniforms at home and their light ones on the road.

Maurice Morris runs with the ball in Seattle's 2007 home uniform.

We Won!

The 2005 season was just a few weeks old when football fans learned just how powerful the Seahawks were. Their offensive line—led by Walter Jones, Steve Hutchinson, and Robbie Tobeck—was creating huge holes, and running back Shaun Alexander blasted through them for long gains. When Matt Hasselbeck dropped back to pass, no one could lay a hand on him. At one point, the Seahawks won 11 games in a row.

The Seahawks finished the regular season with the best record in the NFC. They faced the Washington Redskins in the playoffs. Early in the game, Alexander was tackled hard and suffered a *concussion*. Without their star, the Seahawks asked their linemen to work even harder. They pushed around the Redskins on four scoring drives, and Seattle won 20–10.

For the second time in their history, the Seahawks got ready to play for a chance to go to the Super Bowl. Back in the 1983 season, when the team was still part of the AFC, it had reached the conference championship game. Seattle faced the Oakland Raiders and lost 30–14.

For the Seahawks, this was their first **NFC Championship** game since switching conferences in 2002. Their opponents were the

LEFT: Steve Hutchinson (#76) and Walter Jones (#71), the leaders of Seattle's great offensive line.   **ABOVE**: Matt Hasselbeck points to the fans after a touchdown run against the Washington Redskins.

Go-To Guys

To be a true star in the NFL, you need more than fast feet and a big body. You have to be a "go-to guy"—someone the coach wants on the field at the end of a big game. Seahawks fans have had a lot to cheer about over the years, including these great stars …

THE PIONEERS

STEVE LARGENT   Receiver

• BORN: 9/28/1954   • PLAYED FOR TEAM: 1976 TO 1989

The Seahawks could always count on Steve Largent. Even though he did not have lightning speed, he was very difficult to cover. When a pass

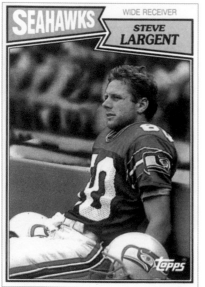

came Largent's way, he never dropped it. In 1995, Largent became the first Seahawk to enter the **Hall of Fame**.

JIM ZORN   Quarterback

• BORN: 5/10/1953   • PLAYED FOR TEAM: 1976 TO 1984

Jim Zorn developed into a good quarterback by earning the trust and respect of his teammates. He worked out as hard as his offensive linemen, and he was just as tough. Zorn led the AFC in passing yards and completions in 1978.

ABOVE: Steve Largent
RIGHT: Dave Krieg

DAVE KRIEG
Quarterback

• BORN: 10/20/1958 • PLAYED FOR TEAM: 1980 TO 1991

Dave Krieg was unknown when he made the Seahawks as a backup in 1980. Three years later, coach Chuck Knox gave him a chance to play, and Krieg led Seattle to the playoffs for the first time. In 1984, Krieg threw 32 touchdown passes and brought the team back to the playoffs.

KENNY EASLEY
Defensive Back

• BORN: 1/15/1959 • PLAYED FOR TEAM: 1981 TO 1987

Kenny Easley was tall, fast, and powerful. He glided around the field to make tackles and interceptions. Easley was the best safety in the NFL until an injury ended his career at the age of 28.

CURT WARNER
Running Back

• BORN: 3/18/1961 • PLAYED FOR TEAM: 1983 TO 1989

Curt Warner loved to carry the ball, and the Seahawks loved to let him do it. He led the AFC in rushing as a rookie and again three years later. Warner had four 1,000-yard seasons in all.

CHRIS WARREN
Running Back

• BORN: 1/24/1968 • PLAYED FOR TEAM: 1990 TO 1997

During the mid-1990s, few running backs were better than Chris Warren. He used his smooth strides to lead the AFC in rushing yards in 1994 and rushing touchdowns in 1995.

MODERN STARS

CORTEZ KENNEDY   Defensive Lineman

• BORN: 8/23/1968   • PLAYED FOR TEAM: 1990 TO 2000

Cortez Kennedy was a huge lineman who could toss blockers aside and then wrap up running backs with his strong arms. He and Sam Adams teamed up to make running up the middle against the Seahawks almost impossible.

JOEY GALLOWAY   Receiver

• BORN: 11/20/1971   • PLAYED FOR TEAM: 1995 TO 1998

Joey Galloway was one of the fastest receivers in the NFL when he played for the Seahawks. The team liked to throw long passes to Galloway and fool the defense by handing off to him, too. In his rookie season, he scored on an 86-yard run.

WALTER JONES   Offensive Lineman

• BORN: 1/19/1974

• FIRST SEASON WITH TEAM: 1997

Many fans believe that Walter Jones is the best player the Seahawks have ever had. His blocking created big holes for Seattle running backs, and his big body and great balance made it very difficult for defenders to reach the quarterback for a sack.

LEFT: Walter Jones
TOP RIGHT: Matt Hasselbeck
BOTTOM RIGHT: Lofa Tatupu

SHAUN ALEXANDER — Running Back

• BORN: 8/30/1977 • PLAYED FOR TEAM: 2000 TO 2007

Few players have ever been as good near the goal line as Shaun Alexander. He led the NFC in touchdowns four times in five seasons and was the the conference's top rusher in 2004 and 2005.

MATT HASSELBECK — Quarterback

• BORN: 9/25/1975 • FIRST SEASON WITH TEAM: 2001

Before Matt Hasselbeck joined the Seahawks, he spent two seasons with the Green Bay Packers backing up Brett Favre. Hasselbeck learned a lot from the star passer. In 2005, Hasselbeck was the NFC's top-rated quarterback and led the Seahawks all the way to the Super Bowl.

LOFA TATUPU — Linebacker

• BORN: 11/15/1982 • FIRST SEASON WITH TEAM: 2005

When the Seahawks drafted Lofa Tatupu, they hoped he would use his speed and intelligence to become a starter on defense. Tatupu had even

bigger dreams. He made the **Pro Bowl** in each of his first three seasons and was named **All-Pro** in 2007.

On the Sidelines

Does a good coach make a big difference in the NFL? Seahawks fans know the answer to that question. A good coach makes all the difference in the world. Seattle's first head coach was Jack Patera. He understood what it took for a new team to **dominate** the battle at the **line of scrimmage**. Seattle had a winning team by its third season.

Patera was followed by Chuck Knox. He believed in a powerful running game. Fans called his *strategy* "Ground Chuck." Knox led the Seahawks to the playoffs for the first time in their history. Seattle was the third team he had taken to the postseason.

After several up-and-down seasons in the 1990s, Seattle hired Mike Holmgren. He was a good judge of talent and a smart coach. Holmgren taught his players how to control the pace of a game and keep the score close until they were ready to make their move. Under Holmgren, the Seahawks made it to the Super Bowl for the first time in team history.

Mike Holmgren gives instructions to quarterback Matt Hasselbeck. Holmgren helped turn Hasselbeck into a Pro Bowl player.

One Great Day

Shaun Alexander loved to score touchdowns. When he got near the goal line, he was almost impossible to stop. The Minnesota Vikings learned this lesson the hard way during the 2002 season. When the Seahawks played the Vikings that year, Alexander was ready for a big day. In his first three games of the season, he had not gained more than 40 yards. Seattle had lost each time.

In the first quarter against Minnesota, Alexander smashed into the end zone on a two-yard run. Later, he scored a 20-yard touchdown. The Seahawks led 17–10 with just over three minutes left in the second quarter when Alexander caught a short pass from Trent Dilfer. Alexander faked out two defenders and ran 80 yards for his third touchdown of the game. It was the longest receiving play of his career.

The 25-year-old running back barely had a chance to catch his breath. The Vikings fumbled the kickoff, and the Seattle offense went back to work. Dilfer handed the ball to Alexander, and he burst through a huge hole and ran untouched into the end zone for a three-yard touchdown.

Shaun Alexander breaks free for a long touchdown against the Minnesota Vikings.

The Seahawks kicked off again, and the Vikings fumbled again. This time, Seattle recovered the ball on the 14 yard line. Alexander jogged back on the field, and on the next play, he ran for his third touchdown in just over one minute.

Alexander's five touchdowns in the first half set an NFL record. Late in the fourth quarter, he had a chance to tie the record of six touchdowns in a game. The Seahawks had the ball on Minnesota's 5 yard line and handed off to Alexander. The Vikings finally tackled him before he reached the end zone. The Seahawks kicked a field goal to make the final score 48–23.

Legend Has It

Which Seahawk had the greatest season ever?

LEGEND HAS IT that Cortez Kennedy did. Shaun Alexander was the NFL's **Most Valuable Player (MVP)** in 2005, but Kennedy may have had an even greater season in 1992. That year, after every game, Seattle's opponents were glad they didn't have to battle Kennedy anymore. He was a one-man tackling machine. It often took three players to block him. When it came time to pick the NFL Defensive Player of the Year, Kennedy was the easy choice. The amazing thing is that Seattle won just twice that season—the top defensive player had never come from a team with such a poor record!

ABOVE: Cortez Kennedy makes a tackle during the 1992 season.
RIGHT: A trading card of Curt Warner, Seattle's great "cutback" runner.

Who was Seattle's best "cutback" runner?

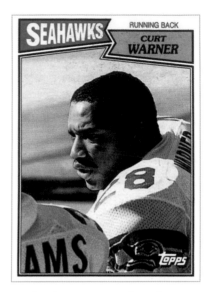

LEGEND HAS IT that Curt Warner was. A good running back is like an *orchestra conductor*. When he moves, everyone follows. When Warner carried the ball in one direction, tacklers would all start moving in the same direction. Warner loved to wait for just the right moment and then cut back sharply in the opposite direction. By the time the defense adjusted, Warner had usually broken free for a big gain.

Did Mike Holmgren once fire himself?

LEGEND HAS IT that he almost did. Holmgren wore two hats for the Seahawks. He was the head coach and the head of the team's business. After the 2004 season, Holmgren "the boss" decided that Holmgren "the coach" had let the team down. Seattle had lost in the playoffs, and Holmgren thought he was to blame. In his mind, the only thing to do was fire the coach. Owner Paul Allen talked him out of it, and the Seahawks went to the Super Bowl the next year!

It Really Happened

Crazy things happen all the time in the NFL, but few things are harder to explain than the 1979 Seahawks. The team was in its fourth year and had just completed its first winning season. Seattle's offense was very good, but its defense was not. After the team lost five of its first seven games, coach Jack Patera decided that he would try anything to keep the defense off the field.

That meant keeping the offense *on* the field. Patera had to **invent** tricky fourth-down plays so his team could avoid punting. The stars of Seattle's "Flying Circus" were Jim Zorn and Steve Largent. Many times during the season, with the Seahawks on the **brink** of disaster, Zorn and Largent connected on incredible pass plays. Zorn would scramble in three different directions, just inches away from his pursuers. Largent would run in loops until he got open. Often, the player guarding him tripped over his own feet. Largent ended up leading the NFL

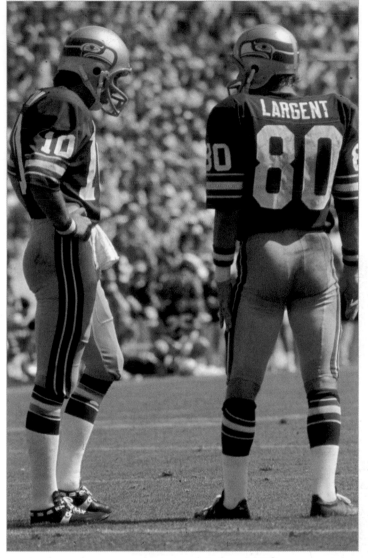

in receiving yards. He averaged almost 20 yards per catch. The Seahawks also tried fake punts and fake field goals. Opponents could never rest, especially on fourth down.

Somehow, Patera's strategy worked. The Seahawks won seven of their final nine games to finish with a 9–7 record. In a game against the Atlanta Falcons, they won with a **quarterback sneak** on fourth down, an **onside kick**, and a long pass to kicker Efren Herrera, who had just faked a field goal. In their final two games, the Seahawks knocked the Denver Broncos out of first place, and then the Oakland Raiders out of the playoffs. It was a season that Seattle fans are still talking about.

Team Spirit

Seattle football fans are famous for their support of the Seahawks. They are noisy and knowledgeable. When the Seahawks are playing a close game at home, the crowd cheers so loudly that opposing players can barely hear each other in the huddle.

In 1984, the Seahawks retired jersey number 12 to honor their fans. The number 12 stands for "12th Man"—which is a nickname that many teams use for their fans. A football team puts 11 players on the field for every play. A loud crowd is like a 12th player. Before each Seahawks game, a celebrity raises a flag with the number 12 on it. This is one of the team's most popular *traditions*.

A newer tradition involves a live hawk named Taima. The bird has been trained to lead the team onto the field before games. Another hawk that appears at Seattle's games is Blitz, a big blue *mascot* that the Seahawks first introduced in 1998. Between games, Blitz visits schools in Washington to help with the team's Ready-Set-Goals reading program.

Seahawks fans wave flags that show their pride in being Seattle's "12th Man."

Timeline

In this timeline, each Super Bowl is listed under the year it was played. Remember that the Super Bowl is held early in the year and is actually part of the previous season. For example, Super Bowl XLII was played on February 3rd, 2008, but it was the championship of the 2007 NFL season.

1976
The Seahawks go 2–12 in their first season.

1983
Curt Warner leads the AFC in rushing as a rookie.

1978
The Seahawks have their first winning season.

1979
Efren Herrera becomes the first Seahawk to score 100 points.

1984
Kenny Easley leads the NFL with 10 interceptions.

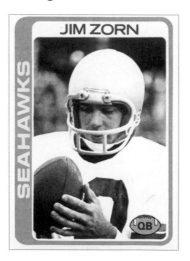

Jim Zorn, a star of the 1978 team.

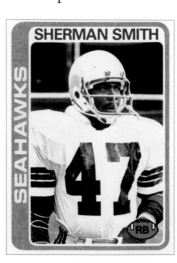

Sherman Smith, Seattle's best runner in the 1970s.

Chris
Warren

Shaun
Alexander

1994
Chris Warren leads the AFC in rushing with 1,545 yards.

1999
The Seahawks win their second AFC West championship.

2005
Shaun Alexander ties a record with 27 rushing touchdowns.

1992
Cortez Kennedy is the NFL's Defensive Player of the Year.

1995
Steve Largent is elected to the Hall of Fame.

2006
The Seahawks reach the Super Bowl for the first time.

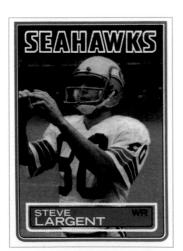

Steve
Largent

Michael Boulware, a star on the Super Bowl team.

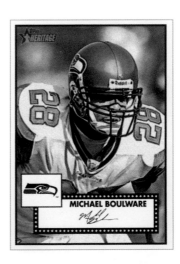

Fun Facts

HOME COOKIN'

The Seahawks were not very polite hosts in 2003. That year, they won all eight of their home games during the regular season.

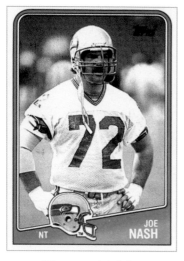

NO ORDINARY JOE

Defensive lineman Joe Nash was one of the most popular players on the Seahawks in the 1980s and 1990s. His specialty was blocking field goals. He knocked down eight kicks during his career.

JUST FOR KICKS

From 1982 to 1990, Norm Johnson was one of the most accurate kickers in the NFL. The fans nicknamed him "Mr. Automatic" because he never seemed to miss a field goal.

MR. 300

In each of his first two playoff games, Matt Hasselbeck threw for more than 300 yards. He became just the third quarterback in NFL history to do this.

THE BOZ

In 1987, the Seahawks signed college superstar Brian Bosworth to the largest rookie contract in NFL history. Unfortunately, an injury ended his career after just three seasons. Bosworth later became a movie actor.

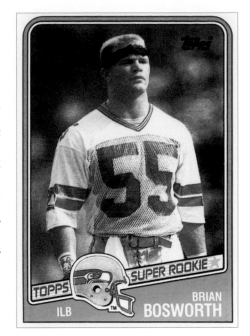

CONFERENCE CALL

The Seahawks are the only team to switch conferences twice. They played in the NFC their first year, moved to the AFC in their second year, and then moved back to the NFC in 2002.

GOAL LINE

Receiver Tommy Kane had some talented teammates on the Seahawks in the 1980s and 1990s. His greatest teammate, however, wore a completely different helmet. He was hockey Hall of Famer Mario Lemieux. They played on the same *Midget League* team as boys in Canada.

LEFT: Joe Nash
ABOVE: Brian Bosworth

Talking Football

"My strongest asset is my desire to work hard and improve."
—*Jim Zorn, on how he became a starting quarterback in the NFL*

"You don't get a chance to have a coach of Mike's **caliber** on your side very often."
—*Paul Allen, on head coach Mike Holmgren*

"I have to smile and pinch myself when I look back over the course of my career here in Seattle."
—*Steve Largent, on how much he loved playing for the Seahawks*

"It's a great feeling to win. I don't like failing in anything. So winning is a great comfort to me."
—*Cortez Kennedy, on what motivated him on the field*

"I'm trying to get to a Super Bowl. That's the only award I care about."

—*Lofa Tatupu, on being a team player*

"You don't get a chance to put a guy on his back too much in this league. So anytime you get a chance to do that, I figure you go ahead and do it."

—*Walter Jones, on why he loves to flatten opponents with "pancake" blocks*

"I was a little bit stubborn when I first got here, had ideas about how I thought things should go and thought I was kind of running the show. And I found out quickly that I was not."

—*Matt Hasselbeck, on learning to play the "Seattle" way*

"I can see things really well. I see holes before they open up, because I can just feel it happening."

—*Shaun Alexander, on why he was especially good near the goal line*

LEFT: Paul Allen and Mike Holmgren
ABOVE: Matt Hasselbeck

For the Record

The great Seahawks teams and players have left their marks on the record books. These are the "best of the best" …

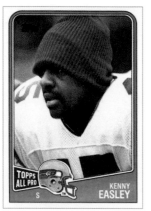

Kenny Easley

Cortez Kennedy

SEAHAWKS AWARD WINNERS

WINNER	AWARD	YEAR
Jack Patera	Coach of the Year	1978
Kenny Easley	Defensive Player of the Year	1984
Chuck Knox	Coach of the Year	1984
Cortez Kennedy	Defensive Player of the Year	1992
Shaun Alexander	Offensive Player of the Year	2005
Shaun Alexander	Most Valuable Player	2005

Shaun Alexander

SEAHAWKS ACHIEVEMENTS

ACHIEVEMENT	YEAR
AFC West Champions	1988
AFC West Champions	1999
NFC West Champions	2004
NFC West Champions	2005
NFC Champions	2005
NFC West Champions	2006
NFC West Champions	2007

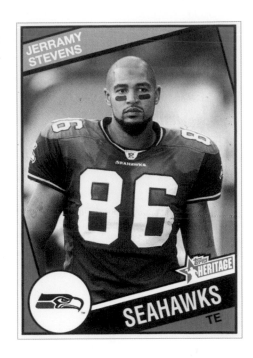

TOP RIGHT: Jerramy Stevens, a star on the 2005 team.

BOTTOM RIGHT: Nate Burleson, a star on the 2007 team.

BELOW: Chuck Knox, the 1984 Coach of the Year.

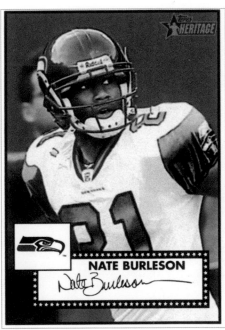

Pinpoints

The history of a football team is made up of many smaller stories. These stories take place all over the map—not just in the city a team calls "home." Match the pushpins on these maps to the Team Facts and you will begin to see the story of the Seahawks unfold!

TEAM FACTS

1 Seattle, Washington—*The team has played here since 1976.*

2 Whittier, California—*Jim Zorn was born here.*

3 Tulsa, Oklahoma—*Steve Largent was born here.*

4 Iola, Wisconsin—*Dave Krieg was born here.*

5 Pasadena, Texas—*Jacob Green was born here.*

6 Wyoming, West Virginia—*Curt Warner was born here.*

7 Chesapeake, Virginia—*Kenny Easley was born here.*

8 Florence, Kentucky—*Shaun Alexander was born here.*

9 Osceola, Arkansas—*Cortez Kennedy was born here.*

10 Aliceville, Alabama—*Walter Jones was born here.*

11 Palatka, Florida—*John L. Williams was born here.*

12 Guadalajara, Mexico—*Efren Herrera was born here.*

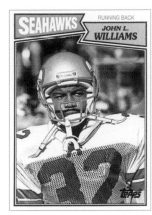

John L. Williams

Play Ball

Football is a sport played by two teams on a field that is 100 yards long. The game is divided into four 15-minute quarters. Each team must have 11 players on the field at all times. The group that has the ball is called the offense. The group trying to keep the offense from moving the ball forward is called the defense.

A football game is made up of a series of "plays." Each play starts and ends with a referee's signal. A play begins when the center snaps the ball between his legs to the quarterback. The quarterback then gives the ball to a teammate, throws (or "passes") the ball to a teammate, or runs with the ball himself. The job of the defense is to tackle the player with the ball or stop the quarterback's pass. A play ends when the ball (or player holding the ball) is "down." The offense must move the ball forward at least 10 yards every four downs. If it fails to do so, the other team is given the ball. If the offense has not made 10 yards after three downs—and does not want to risk losing the ball—it can kick (or "punt") the ball to make the other team start from its own end of the field.

At each end of a football field is a goal line, which divides the field from the end zone. A team must run or pass the ball over the goal line to score a touchdown, which counts for six points. After scoring a touchdown, a team can try a short kick for one "extra point," or try again to run or pass across the goal line for two points. Teams can score three points from anywhere on the field by kicking the ball between the goal posts. This is called a field goal.

The defense can score two points if it tackles a player while he is in his own end zone. This is called a safety. The defense can also score points by taking the ball away from the offense and crossing the opposite goal line for a touchdown. The team with the most points after 60 minutes is the winner.

Football may seem like a very hard game to understand, but the more you play and watch football, the more "little things" you are likely to notice. The next time you are at a game, look for these plays:

 PLAY LIST

BLITZ—A play where the defense sends extra tacklers after the quarterback. If the quarterback sees a blitz coming, he passes the ball quickly. If he does not, he can end up at the bottom of a very big pile!

DRAW—A play where the offense pretends it will pass the ball, and then gives it to a running back. If the offense can "draw" the defense to the quarterback and his receivers, the running back should have lots of room to run.

FLY PATTERN—A play where a team's fastest receiver is told to "fly" past the defensive backs for a long pass. Many long touchdowns are scored on this play.

SQUIB KICK—A play where the ball is kicked a short distance on purpose. A squib kick is used when the team kicking off does not want the other team's fastest player to catch the ball and run with it.

SWEEP—A play where the ball carrier follows a group of teammates moving sideways to "sweep" the defense out of the way. A good sweep gives the runner a chance to gain a lot of yards before he is tackled or forced out of bounds.

Glossary

AFC WEST—A division for teams that play in the western part of the country.

ALL-PRO—An honor given to the best players at their position at the end of each season.

AMERICAN FOOTBALL CONFERENCE (AFC)—One of two groups of teams that make up the NFL. The winner of the AFC plays the winner of the NFC in the Super Bowl.

BLOCKERS—Players who protect the ball carrier with their bodies.

DRAFTED—Chosen from a group of the best college players. The NFL draft is held each spring.

FUMBLE—A ball that is dropped by the player carrying it.

HALL OF FAME—The museum in Canton, Ohio, where football's greatest players are honored. A player voted into the Hall of Fame is sometimes called a "Hall of Famer."

INTERCEPTION—A pass that is caught by the defensive team.

LINE OF SCRIMMAGE—The imaginary line that separates the offense and defense before each play begins.

MOST VALUABLE PLAYER (MVP)—The award given each year to the league's best player; also given to the best player in the Super Bowl and Pro Bowl.

NATIONAL FOOTBALL CONFERENCE (NFC)—One of two groups of teams that make up the NFL. The winner of the NFC plays the winner of the AFC in the Super Bowl.

NATIONAL FOOTBALL LEAGUE (NFL)—The league that started in 1920 and is still operating today.

NFC CHAMPIONSHIP—The game played to determine which NFC team will go to the Super Bowl.

NFC WEST—A division for teams that play in the western part of the country.

ONSIDE KICK—A short kickoff that the kicking team tries to recover.

PLAYOFFS—The games played after the season to determine which teams play in the Super Bowl.

PRO BOWL—The NFL's all-star game, played after the Super Bowl.

PROFESSIONAL—A player or team that plays a sport for money.

QUARTERBACK SNEAK—A play where the quarterback keeps the ball and tries to "sneak" past the defensive line.

ROOKIE—A player in his first season.

SACKED—Tackled the quarterback behind the line of scrimmage.

SUPER BOWL—The championship of football, played between the winners of the NFC and AFC.

OTHER WORDS TO KNOW

BRINK—Edge.

CALIBER—A level of ability.

CONCUSSION—A head injury that affects the brain.

CONTENDER—A team that competes for a championship.

DECADE—A period of 10 years; also specific periods, such as the 1950s.

DOMINATE—Completely control through the use of power.

INTENSE—Very strong or very deep.

INVENT—Create through clever thinking.

ORCHESTRA CONDUCTOR—The leader of a large group of musicians.

MASCOT—An animal or person believed to bring a group good luck.

MIDGET LEAGUE—A level of hockey for young players.

RIVALS—Extremely emotional competitors.

STRATEGY—A plan or method for succeeding.

TAILBONE—The bone that protects the base of the spine.

TRADITIONS—Beliefs or customs that are handed down from generation to generation.

Places to Go

ON THE ROAD

SEATTLE SEAHAWKS
800 Occidental Avenue South
Seattle, Washington 98134
(425) 827-9777

THE PRO FOOTBALL HALL OF FAME
2121 George Halas Drive NW
Canton, Ohio 44708
(330) 456-8207

ON THE WEB

THE NATIONAL FOOTBALL LEAGUE   www.nfl.com
  • *Learn more about the National Football League*

THE SEATTLE SEAHAWKS   www.seahawks.com
  • *Learn more about the Seahawks*

THE PRO FOOTBALL HALL OF FAME   www.profootballhof.com
  • *Learn more about football's greatest players*

ON THE BOOKSHELF

To learn more about the sport of football, look for these books at your library or bookstore:

  • Fleder, Rob–Editor. *The Football Book*. New York, New York: Sports Illustrated Books, 2005.

  • Kennedy, Mike. *Football*. Danbury, Connecticut: Franklin Watts, 2003.

  • Savage, Jeff. *Play by Play Football*. Minneapolis, Minnesota: Lerner Sports, 2004.

Index

The Team

MARK STEWART has written more than 20 books on football, and over 100 sports books for kids. He grew up in New York City during the 1960s rooting for the Giants and Jets, and now takes his two daughters, Mariah and Rachel, to watch them play in their home state of New Jersey. Mark

comes from a family of writers. His grandfather was Sunday Editor of *The New York Times* and his mother was Articles Editor of *The Ladies' Home Journal* and *McCall's*. Mark has profiled hundreds of athletes over the last 20 years. He has also written several books about New York and New Jersey. Mark is a graduate of Duke University, with a degree in History. He lives with his daughters and wife Sarah overlooking Sandy Hook, New Jersey.

JASON AIKENS is the Collections Curator at the Pro Football Hall of Fame. He is responsible for the preservation of the Pro Football Hall of Fame's collection of artifacts and memorabilia and obtaining new donations of memorabilia from current players and NFL teams. Jason has a Bachelor of Arts in History from Michigan State University and a Master's in History from Western Michigan University where he concentrated on sports history. Jason

has been working for the Pro Football Hall of Fame since 1997; before that he was an intern at the College Football Hall of Fame. Jason's family has roots in California and has been following the St. Louis Rams since their days in Los Angeles, California. He lives with his wife Cynthia and their daughter Angelina in Canton, Ohio.